BUSINESS
CHINA

BUSINESS
CHINA

A Practical Guide to Understanding Chinese Business Culture

Peggy Kenna   **Sondra Lacy**

Printed on recyclable paper

PASSPORT BOOKS
a division of *NTC Publishing Group*
Lincolnwood, Illinois USA

Library of Congress Cataloging-in-Publication Data

Kenna, Peggy.
  Business China: a practical guide to understanding Chinese business
culture / Peggy Kenna, Sondra Lacy.
    p.   cm.
  ISBN 0-8442-3556-3
  1. Corporate culture—China.   2. Business etiquette—China.
  I. Lacy, Sondra.   II. Title.
HD58.7.K45   1994
395' .52'0951—dc20   93—42811
                                              CIP

1996 Printing

Published by Passport Books, a division of NTC Publishing Group.
4255 West Touhy Avenue, Lincolnwood, (Chicago) Illinois 60646-1975, U.S.A.
©1994 by NTC Publishing Group. All rights reserved.
No part of this work may be reproduced, stored in a retrieval system
or transmitted in any form or by any means,
electronic or mechanical, including photocopying and recording or otherwise
without the prior permission of NTC Publishing Group.
Manufactured in the United States of America.

  5 6 7 8 9 0 VP 9 8 7 6 5 4 3 2

Contents

Peggy Kenna is a communication specialist working with foreign-born professionals in the American workplace. She provides cross-cultural training and consultation services to companies conducting business internationally. She is also a certified speech and language pathologist who specializes in accent modification. Peggy lives in Tempe, Arizona.

Sondra Lacy is a certified communications specialist who teaches American communication skills to foreign-born professionals in the American workplace. She also provides cross-cultural training and consultation services to companies conducting business internationally. Sondra lives in Scottsdale, Arizona.

Business China is an invaluable tool for thousands of entrepreneurs, businesspeople, corporate executives, technicians, and salespeople seeking to develop lasting business relationships in China.

The book provides a fast, easy way for you to become acquainted with business practices and protocol to help you increase your chances for success in China. You will discover the secrets of doing business internationally while improving your interpersonal communication skills.

Let this book work for you.

> Pam Del Duca
> President/CEO
> The DELSTAR Group
> Scottsdale, Arizona

 Entrepreneur Of The Year®
Award Recipient

Welcome to Business China

Business China offers a smooth and problem-free transition between the American and Chinese business cultures.

This pocket-size book contains information you need when traveling in the People's Republic of China or doing business with Chinese colleagues. It explains the differences in business culture you will encounter in areas such as:

- Business etiquette
- Communication style
- Problem solving and decision making
- Meetings and presentation style

Business China gets you started on the right track and challenges you to seek ways to improve your success in the global marketplace by understanding cultural differences in the ways people communicate and do business with each other.

Successful international companies are able to adapt to the business styles acceptable in other countries and by other nationalities, based on their knowledge and awareness of key cultural differences. These differences, if not acknowledged and addressed, can interfere in successful communication and can adversely affect the success of any business attempting to expand internationally.

Business China is designed to overcome such difficulties by comparing the American culture with the culture of China. Identifying appropriate behavior in one's own culture can make it easier to adapt to that of the country with which you are doing business. With this in mind, the book's unique parallel layout allows an at-a-glance comparison of Chinese business practices with those of the United States.

Practical and easy to use, *Business China* will help you win the confidence of Chinese colleagues and achieve common business goals.

The global business environment today is a multicultural one. While general business considerations are essentially the same the world over, business styles differ greatly from country to country. What is customary and appropriate in one country may be considered unusual or even offensive in another. The increasingly competitive environment calls for an individual approach to each national market. The success of your venture outside your home market depends largely upon preparation. The American style of business is not universally accepted. Yet we send our employees, executives, salespeople, technicians to negotiate or carry out contracts with little or no understanding of the cultural differences in the ways people communicate and do business with each other. How many business deals have been lost because of this cultural myopia?

Globalization is a process which is drawing people together from all nations of the world into a single community linked by the vast network of communication technologies. Technological breakthroughs in the past two decades have made instant communication by individuals around the world an affordable reality.

As these technological advances continue to open up and expand the dialogue among members of the world community, the need for effective international and interpersonal communication has accelerated.

When change occurs as dramatically and rapidly as we have witnessed in the past decade, many people throughout the world are being forced to quickly learn and adapt to unfamiliar ways of doing things. Some actually welcome change and the opportunities it presents, while others are reluctant to give up familiar ways of doing things. History proves that cultures are slow to change. But individuals who are mentally prepared to accept change and deal with differences can successfully understand and adapt to cultures very different from their own.

A culture develops when individuals have common experiences and share their reactions to these experiences by communicating with other members of their society.

Over time, communication becomes the vehicle by which cultural beliefs and values are developed, shared and transmitted from one generation to the next. Communication and culture are mutually dependent.

Effective communication between governments or international businesses requires more than being able to speak the language fluently or relying on expert interpreters. Understanding the language is only the first step. Identifying and accepting the behaviors, customs and attitudes of other cultures is also required to bring harmony and success to the worldwide business and political arena.

The importance of the influence of one's native culture on the way one approaches life cannot be overstated. Each country's cultural beliefs and values are reflected in its people's idea of the "right" way to live and behave.

In general, businesspeople who practice low-key, non-adversarial, win/win techniques in doing business abroad tend to be most successful. Knowing what your company wants to achieve, its bottom line, and also understanding the objectives of the other party and helping to accommodate them in the business transaction are necessary for developing long-term, international business relationships.

Often, representatives from American companies, for example, have difficulty doing business with *each other*, even when they speak the same language and share a common culture. Consider how much more difficult it is to do business with people from different cultures who speak different languages.

Success in the international business arena will not be easy for those who do not take steps to gain the skills necessary to be global players. The language barrier is an obvious problem.

Equally important will be negotiation skills, as well as an understanding of and adaptation to the social and business etiquette of the foreign country. Americans have a reputation for failing to appreciate this.

In other words, businesspeople doing business abroad will get off to a good start if they remember to do the following:

- Listen closely; understand the verbal and non-verbal communications.

- Focus on mutual interests, not differences.

- Nurture long-term relationships.

- Emphasize quality. Be prepared to defend the quality of your products and services, and the quality of your business relationship.

China is the world's oldest and most pervasive bureaucracy. Much of the country is just emerging from feudalism with Communist ideology on top. The business structure is in the middle of "reforms" that are attempting to create a new economic order. To do business in China takes a lot of patience and perserverance. The Chinese are known as tough negotiators and it can take months or even years to arrange an investment or contract.

Confucius has had a profound influence in China. He stressed obedience and respect for authority. China has had a very strict code of behavior in effect for 2,000 years. Carefully prescribed forms of behavior cover virtually every aspect of conduct. The higher one is on the social scale, the more meticulous and demanding the rules of behavior.

Devotion to the family is strong. Family life generally takes precedence over loyalty to the state. The government has taken strong measures in recent years to limit family size and population growth.

China's GNP is the sixth largest in the world but it has one of the lowest per capita incomes because it is the most populous country in the world. One quarter of the world's population is Chinese. Within China there are at least 56 ethnic groups.

Agriculture is the foundation of the economy and remains a top priority; they are also interested in energy, transportation, communications and raw materials. They have the potential to become a major industrial power due to their abundant natural resources.

China is a tough place for any Westerner to do business. Western women will find acceptance but even though equality between sexes is a key Communist tenet, few women reach key positions.

You must have an invitation to do business in China. This may take a year or more to obtain. So patience is necessary. And China is still more a potential than an actual market.

China's future is politically unstable. Power rests with a small group of Communists in their eighties. When they die, political unrest could result. How future leaders will deal with reforms is at present unclear.

United States

■ *Belief in competition*

Americans believe that competition fosters creativity and contributes to high performance. One person is usually given power to make the final decision and bear all responsibility. Americans also believe that all decisions should be based on facts and that they should be "upfront" with these facts.

■ *Individual oriented*

Individual Americans can behave in widely different ways. Americans are very diverse and there are few real norms for behavior. Because of this, the Chinese tend to find Americans puzzling and don't know what to expect.

Americans value individual recognition and feel group/team membership to be only temporary. People gain their identity through their individual achievements.

■ *Belief in harmony*

The Chinese believe that everything must be in harmony for the world to be in balance and that competition leads to disharmony. They take a long-range view of things and believe change is disruptive and that non-action is better than action.

■ *Group oriented*

The Chinese focus on the group instead of the individual; they don't like to be singled out as having unique qualities. The Chinese also do not accept individual responsibility. People gain their identity from the family, the group or the company.

Because the Chinese language has no word for "privacy," individuals in China do nothing on their own; they always seek the opinion and support of their group. Strangers can be treated with indifference or even contempt.

United States

■ *Relationships are short term*

To Americans, business relationships are not personal. Friendships are formed very quickly and can be dissolved just as fast. Americans generally believe time should not be wasted on unnecessary conversation and social niceties.

Americans tend to have little problem meeting strangers and they are inclined to trust the other party until proven wrong.

In general, anger is an acceptable emotion to Americans. They believe that properly channeled, anger can get to the heart of problems and thus allow a solution to be found.

■ *Relationships important*

Person to person communication is critical to the Chinese. Unless they know you personally and have acknowledged your existence, you do not exist and no amount of letter writing, telexing or faxing will do any good. Friendships are formed slowly but last a lifetime.

Human relationships are very important to the Chinese. They believe the time should be taken to build solid relationships, especially before doing business. They have a great respect for feeling and dislike using the word "I." A person's reputation and standing in the social structure is very important. The Chinese depend on a vast network of social relationships to get things done.

At every encounter the Chinese will be studying your temperament and sincerity. If they decide they don't like you, they won't do business with you.

Anger is very unacceptable to them. They dislike being challenged or having answers demanded from them.

United States

■ *Cause and effect logic*

Americans decide what to do on the basis of what effect an action will have; they look at a problem in terms of what they might do to find a solution.

Americans believe the most productive thinking is linear and rational in nature; it is based on concrete evidence and facts.

■ *Admire fluency*

Americans are great talkers and tend to become uncomfortable with too much silence. Some also believe it is all right to boast and occasionally exaggerate.

■ *Truth is absolute*

Americans believe that truth is absolute and does not depend on circumstances. A fact is either true or false. They believe that what is true for one person is true for everyone. Americans prefer to use ambiguous expressions such as "it is interesting" rather than tell a lie to someone they don't want to hurt. They also tend to feel that saying nothing is better than telling a lie just to make a person feel better.

■ *Logic of relationship*

The Chinese decide what to do on the basis of whether the action fits the existing plan; they look at a problem to see how it fits into already established, ongoing patterns. They do not debate issues on the basis of right/wrong, fair/unfair. They base their actions on circumstances, not principles.

■ *Ample use of silence*

The Chinese believe that it is better to talk too little than too much. They also believe that it is very important to be consistent in what you say.

■ *Truth is relative*

The Chinese believe that truth is relative to circumstances and human obligations. Telling another what they believe that person wants to hear instead of the absolute truth is considered part of hospitality. Nothing must be allowed to disrupt surface harmony of the individual, therefore they may give an answer just to please the listener.

United States

■ *Face saving less important*

Western cultural values are based on the Judeo-Christian ethic which is an internal ethic based on religion.

To Americans accuracy is important but errors are tolerated. Admitting mistakes is seen as a sign of maturity. They believe you can learn from failure and therefore encourage risk taking.

Americans believe criticism should be objective; however, all criticism should be done with tact. Actions, not persons, may be criticized. Job related criticism rarely affects a person's private life.

When Americans want to understand a point, they will ask clarifying questions or even say "I don't understand, will you explain it to me, please." Most Americans acknowledge when they don't know something.

■ *Face saving important*

Chinese values are based on human feelings and not on religion. They feel it is very important to never put someone in the position of having to admit a mistake or failure and to never criticize or ridicule what they are doing. To save face, a Chinese might withhold information, color information, avoid commitments and responsibility, cover up or just do nothing. The need for revenge is common when someone loses face.

It is important for a foreigner to phrase questions in a straightforward manner and to make sure the other person understands as the Chinese do not like to admit lack of understanding. Foreigners should also not admit to the Chinese when they don't know something as it will cause them to lose face with the Chinese. If a foreigner loses face, the Chinese will no longer do business with them. And it takes many years to overcome the problems caused by a loss of face.

United States

■ *Direct and to the point*

Americans prefer people to say what they mean. They are uncomfortable with ambiguousness and don't like to have to "fill in the blanks." Americans feel that direct questioning is the best way to get information.

Americans tend to be very straightforward and unreserved and can be seen by others as brusque and not interested enough in human relationships.

Americans are generally frank and open and will tell you if they can or cannot accomplish a task. They will tell you "no" if they are not going to be able to fulfill a request. They feel that direct answers, even if they are negative, are the most efficient.

Americans like to confront problems head on also. They want to find the cause and then do something to solve the problem as quickly as possible.

■ *Indirect and ambiguous*

Since the Chinese are afraid of losing face, they will not tell you when they don't understand. They will also tend to hedge their answers if they know the listener won't like the answer. Frankness is not appreciated by the Chinese. Direct questioning is seen as rude.

Negative answers are also avoided as they cause loss of face, disharmony and are rude. The Chinese believe politeness is more important than frankness so they will not say "no" directly. They may say something like, "I'll see what I can do" or "I'll do my best," which usually means "no" but leaves things open so you can reopen the issue at a later time. If they say something is "not so convenient," it means they need to obtain permission and this takes time.

They also dislike confronting problems directly and tend to go around the issue which can be frustrating for Americans.

The Chinese language (Mandarin) is so terse that the listener needs much imagination to "fill in the gaps."

United States

■ *Direct eye contact*

Direct eye contact is very important to Americans since they need to see the non verbal cues the speaker is giving. The eyes are considered a valuable source of information and attitudes being conveyed.

Americans like to stand about 30 inches or arm's length apart. Limited touching (such as someone's arm) is tolerated in the workplace. Handshakes are always acceptable. Otherwise touching is reserved for special friends and family members.

■ *"Yes" means agreement*

Americans look for clues such as nodding of the head or verbal clues such as "yes" or "uh huh" in order to determine if their arguments are succeeding.

■ *Avoid direct eye contact*

The Chinese consider that holding the gaze of another person is rude and disrespectful.

In business situations the Chinese like more physical distance than Americans and generally, dislike touching.

■ *"Yes" means "I hear you"*

The Chinese do not judge information given to them; they only nod or say "yes" to indicate they are listening to what you are saying. They are not indicating agreement with you.

Leadership/Status

United States

■ *Independent*

Americans expect people to express their opinions openly, and in matters of public policy or group decision making the majority rules. It is considered quite acceptable to question authority figures.

Americans are procedures oriented and like direct specific work orders. Each person has a well defined function in a company.

■ *Status*

To Americans power is more important than maturity and status. Power is not always determined by title, maturity or education; it can be determined by force of personality and political connections. Also, acquiring material wealth is seen as a sign of success. One's position in life is achieved through individual effort.

■ *Revere authority and order*

The delegation of authority and areas of responsibility must be absolutely clear. The Chinese want to know exactly who is responsible for what and who has exactly what kind of authority.

Those in authority cannot admit lack of knowledge or mistakes as that would cause them to "lose face." They also may feel that to learn and accept new ideas will cause them to lose face. Questioning authority figures is not acceptable. In order not to make a manager lose face, employees may not inform that manager of problems or make suggestions for improving operations. The Chinese have a large group of middle management but it is important to get to the top level as quickly as possible as that is where decisions are made.

■ *Status*

Maturity (age) is essential. A young man automatically stands lower on the status scale. Seniority and personal connections are more important than title. One's position in life is achieved through family and connections.

Education is a status symbol, especially if obtained from a well known institution.

United States

■ *Like to debate*

Americans believe debate and argument bring out valid points and can result in a better decision. They also believe that it is possible to disagree with someone but not attack them personally. They feel that any interpersonal conflicts between people should be discussed directly.

■ *Individual decision makers*

Individual decision making is often seen as the most efficient method to use. One person is usually given power to make the final decision and bear all responsibility. Decisions tend to go from the top down; however, decision makers are found at all levels depending on the importance of the decision. Lower levels often get a chance to provide input. Americans believe that those closest to a problem should have input in determining the solution.

Americans assume that at some time in their careers, they will be criticized. They will accept that criticism but they also realize that no one likes it.

■ *Dislike confrontation*

To directly disagree with the Chinese is considered very rude. They do not separate issues from persons. The Chinese are expert at "passing the buck." It never stops.

It is considered polite to act humble but often this is not an indication of how they really feel.

■ *Collective responsibility*

Decisions are made by people in authority but responsibility for the decision is born by the entire group.

It takes a long time for the Chinese to arrive at decisions. The lines of decision-making authority are far from clear. It is wise to discount no one.

An ambitious Chinese strives to be an energetic and intelligent conformist. Bosses are expected to be arbitrary and act without explanation. The Chinese don't want to stand out. Individuals are not expected to give their opinions; they are expected to accept the thinking of those in authority. The Chinese do not want to expose themselves to criticism.

United States

■ *Individual workers*

Lifetime loyalty to a company is no longer considered a major virtue. Americans' loyalty is to self and career. In American companies relationships can cross boundaries of rank and seniority.

Management practices in the U.S. place a distinct organizational structure upon the employees and the employer. Productivity is expected of all and managers delegate projects to be completed to workers in the organization.

■ *Work in teams*

Americans work fairly well in teams. Teams are both competitive and cooperative and there is communication between teams. One person can be a "star" on a team but expected not to act like one.

■ *Work unit system*

Individual Chinese are assigned to a work unit which they basically cannot leave. To show any sign of individual ambition or independent thought or action can bring demotion and a permanent black mark on one's work record.

The most effective management is to treat employees like a family. To carry out a project it is important to gain the confidence of production personnel and supervisors.

■ *Teams don't work*

The Chinese tend not to work well in teams since no one wants to take the initiative. And they tend to squabble.

The Chinese feel very strongly that no one should stand out. Extreme pressure is placed on individuals to remain submerged in the crowd, not to be aggressive or more ambitious than others. Teams need continual supervision and follow-up. Foreigners need to be completely honest and forthright about what they expect of the Chinese.

United States

■ *Planning important*

Americans believe it is important to plan for and anticipate the future. Much time and effort is spent in American companies in planning concepts and establishing procedures to carry out a plan. Success or failure is dependent on the agreed upon plan. Planning is usually top down but it can be bottom up. Good planning requires interpersonal skills. Planning tends to be short term.

■ *Like detailed legal agreements*

Americans like detailed contracts They like to spell out all contingencies and then sign on the bottom line. Action plans and timelines are part of the agreement.

■ *Planning long term*

China has the world's oldest and most entrenched bureaucracy. The bureaucracy is always structured top down. The Chinese have a fondness for strategic long-range planning. And their plans often have very little flexibility.

Decision making is slow in China as all decisions must work their way through a very cumbersome bureaucracy.

■ *Contracts*

The Chinese prefer vague agreements which can be adjusted later as needed. But if problems occur, they take a legalistic view and do not feel bound by anything not explicitly stated in the contract. Contracts should be as specific as possible. Most problems will arise after the contract is signed. Anyone doing business with the Chinese should take notes during negotiations and make sure they see you taking notes.

Most contracts must be approved by the appropriate political organizations. And departments within the government do not always communicate with each other, which makes getting anything approved more difficult.

Punctuality

United States

■ *Linear time*

Westerners view time as a steady, straight progression. There is a past, a present and a future; when a moment is gone, it is gone forever.

Americans tend to be very punctual. Business days are usually divided into segments to be completed. There is a beginning time and ending time for each segment of the day. Therefore, it is very important that each segment begin on time or the whole day can be thrown off.

■ *Time is money*

Americans want to accomplish a job with minimum expenditure of time and effort. They feel that it is important to get a product to market as soon as possible to gain the competitive advantage.

Planning and implementation tend to be very quick. This can sometimes result in problems but failure is allowed because it is felt that any problems or mistakes can be fixed as they arise.

■ *Pragmatic about time*

The Chinese view time in very long terms; their civilization and country is over 2,000 years old. Time is much more fluid to them and they look at the long (i.e., 500 years) view. They don't understand the concept of doing things promptly and feel Americans are much too impatient. The Chinese will often use this impatience against Americans in negotiating with them.

However, the Chinese tend to be punctual about attending meetings, etc.

■ *Use time as a weapon*

Americans can get impatient and the Chinese will use this to their advantage. To let the Chinese know that you have a deadline and need to get back home accomplishes nothing. If they say you should come back in a week, this is exactly what they mean.

To work with the Chinese, it is important that you not expect quick profits. The Chinese want a sense that you'll be around for awhile.

United States

■ *Use as communication tool*

Some meetings are brainstorming meetings; some are to disseminate information; some are to discuss, defend and decide.

Americans like to get down to business right away since meetings are usually tightly scheduled and have a fixed agenda. A meeting may be adjourned before all business is completed. Americans also like to leave with some kind of action plan.

Meetings can become very heated with a number of confrontations and disagreements to be resolved.

■ *Use to disseminate information*

During a meeting only the leader speaks. All differences of opinion have been hashed out before the meeting. The Chinese also expect that the opposing team will have only one spokesperson and that any others in the delegation will not contradict the spokesperson. Individualistic Westerners often find this difficult.

When entering a meeting room, the highest ranking person on the team leads the group in. The Chinese like to have foreigners do the same thing so they will know the hierarchy.

The Chinese want to control every aspect of meetings from first greetings and introductions, to order of seating, to content of discussions, to how they are conducted.

The Chinese also don't jump right into business. They want to begin with appropriate introductory conversation, getting to know each other.

United States

■ *Presentations*

Americans tend to have a projecting style of presentation. They will often combine informative and persuasive styles as an efficient method of presentation. They attempt to persuade the audience to make a decision or take an action at the same time as they provide information. They consider this an effective and efficient use of time.

Americans also believe in the "hard sell" and "quick close" approach to selling.

They expect the audience to ask questions and to test the presenter's knowledge. Presenters expect to defend their opinions.

■ *Presentations*

The Chinese practice the soft sell and the hard buy. Their discussions and questions will be endless, repetitive and detailed; they are checking to see if your answers are consistent.

When making a presentation to the Chinese, it is important to be very knowledgeable about your own products, your competitors, about the market and about your organization.

If you are introducing a new technology to the Chinese, they will ask many detailed questions about this new technology but they won't guarantee you a deal in return. They feel that since they are a poor country, it is only fair that they get all the technology they can. If you are dealing with the Chinese, you must decide how much technology you are willing to divulge.

Negotiating

United States

■ *Task oriented*

Americans are highly task oriented. They are good at taking responsibility and getting things done. They are more interested in the technical aspects of negotiation than in building relationships.

Americans are very open and direct in their communication. They like to deal with differences directly and tend to "lay their cards on the table" in order to resolve issues.

Americans have a tendency to negotiate alone or in teams of less than five people rather than in larger teams.

Americans will complete the negotiations and do not expect a personal relationship with obligations beyond the business transaction. Americans separate business relationships from personal relationships.

■ *Relationship oriented*

To the Chinese, as all Asians, the human element is a dominant factor in business. They feel this element cannot be removed from business. They like to create a sense of friendship and obligation. They use protocol, banquets, etc., to overwhelm. They will go to great lengths to learn food, music preferences,etc., in order to create a sense of friendship.

However, in China, friendship also implies obligation. For their friendship, they will expect concessions. Favors and obligations are weighed very carefully and accounts are strictly kept.

To avoid becoming too overwhelmed, it is best to perform small favors for the Chinese and thus put them in your debt.

The Chinese are single-minded and highly disciplined in pursuit of their own interests. They are distrustful of impersonal or legalistic negotiations.

The Chinese may withhold information and reveal as little as possible to try and put the other side at a disadvantage.

The Chinese always negotiate in large teams and never individually or in small groups.

United States

■ *Legalistic*

Americans are very legalistic and like detailed contracts with all contingencies spelled out. These contracts are fairly inflexible and expected to be adhered to. Contracts are considered very important and have full backing of the American legal system.

■ *Impatient*

Americans like fast paced negotiations and tend to be impatient. This impatience can lead Americans to make unnecessary concessions.

■ *Prefer vague contracts*

The Chinese prefer contracts that do not have too many details as they feel all issues in a contract are still subject to negotiation afterwards. The important thing is to build the relationship. The Chinese do not feel that strict compliance to a contract is mandatory.

The Chinese are meticulous note-takers however and will throw your words back at you later. It is important to maintain a consistent position and take notes at all times.

■ *Use time to their advantage*

The Chinese negotiating position is arrived at in advance and not subject to revision. If a stalemate is reached, they must withdraw and reach a new consensus. This requires patience; there may be long periods of time when nothing seems to happen. They are determining their new position.

United States

■ *Bargaining*

Americans tend to make concessions grudgingly at all times. They are not hagglers. They usually bargain for clear-cut goals such as price, quality or delivery date.

■ *Decision making*

Decisions during negotiations do not always need to be made by executives but can often be made by lower level managers; consensus is not necessary either.

■ *Bargaining*

The Chinese are very practiced and tough negotiators. They can also be very blunt and outspoken. They study Western nonverbal signals in order to gain an advantage.

The Chinese negotiating technique is to keep the other side off balance and defensive, such as "shaming" them into concessions. It is very difficult to negotiate when constantly defending yourself. The Chinese also use the feelings of friendship they have built to their advantage. They will use the friendliest member of the team to apply pressure to the rest of the team.

Foreigners must know their bottom line as the Chinese like to get sizeable concessions.

■ *Decision making*

Decisions are finally made only at the upper levels. Decision making can be very slow since it must work its way through a cumbersome bureaucracy. Chinese negotiators seldom have the authority to make decisions. They usually need to consult with colleagues and superiors before a new position can be agreed upon.

All conversations at lower levels are reported upward through the hierarchy so all team members should be careful of what they say.

Negotiating

United States

■ *Swift*

Americans like negotiations to be fast-paced. They also usually attack issues sequentially, resolving one issue at a time. They want to get to the details quickly and then conclude a contract.

■ *Summary*

Americans tend to have limited knowledge of other cultures. This can become a major obstacle in concluding deals with other countries.

Americans tend to prefer negotiating alone rather in teams. This can become overwhelming especially if the other side has a large team.

Americans often emphasize the short-term. Many other countries, including the Chinese, want to know what the long-term effects will be.

Americans usually emphasize content over relationships. In many countries, including China, relationships are very highly valued.

Americans emphasis on legalistic contracts and their constant deference to lawyers are seen as an insult in many countries.

■ *Long-term*

Entering into a contract with the Chinese is time consuming. When negotiating, the Chinese usually proceed as follows:

1. Create a relationship.
2. Assess your intentions and limits.
3. Withdraw or conclude an agreement.

The second stage can take months or even years. The third stage is reached when they start becoming more concrete about details.

■ *Summary*

The highest ranking member of the team should enter the room first and this same person should always be the spokesperson. Lower ranking members of the team should never interrupt the leader.

Consider bringing your own interpreter along. This can lead to more accurate assessment of what is happening. It can also prevent unintentional loss of face.

Know exactly what you hope to accomplish and how much technology are you willing to give away. And remember that intellectual property has no protection in Chinese law.

Remember that the huge Chinese market is still more potential than actual.

Chinese Business Etiquette

- Direct your first greeting to the senior person in the other group; your group should line up by seniority so they know how you each fit into the business.

- If people greet you with applause, return the applause.

- Do not use first names; use titles. Give rank its due.

- Dress modestly and conservatively.

- Avoid jokes; the Chinese will not know if you are serious or joking.

- Don't let your subordinates interrupt you.

- Giving modest gifts is common.

- Business cards should be presented with both hands. Have your cards printed in both English and Chinese.

- The Chinese will be judging you on every aspect of your professional and personal demeanor. You should play up your affluence and importance.

- Banquets are an important way to start establishing relationships. Business is not discussed and etiquette is very precise.

Chinese Gestures

- Point with your open hand, not with one finger.
- Any type of touching is uncommon.
- When the Chinese are surprised or dismayed by something, they often show this by sucking air quickly and audibly through their lips and teeth.
- To beckon someone, the palm faces down and the fingers are moved in a scratching motion.
- Use the "thumbs up" signal to mean OK.
- Posture is important; don't slouch.
- Bow or shake hands when introduced to someone.
- When conversing, the Chinese tend to stand closer to each other than Americans do.
- In large cities, direct eye contact is uncommon. However, in smaller towns a foreigner may be the object of much curiosity and be stared at.
- Pushing and shoving in stores or when boarding buses and trains is common and not considered rude.

Effective communication, both verbal and non-verbal, means that the sending and processing of information between people, countries and businesses is understood, examined, interpreted, and responded to in some way. Any factor that causes a barrier or eliminates the successful transmission of information is defined as a communication interference.

- **Environmental interference** is an actual physical disturbance in the environment such as power outage, unregulated temperatures, a person or group talking very loud, etc.

- **Physiological interference** can be a hearing loss, laryngitis, illness, stuttering, neurological or organic deficit, etc.

- **Semantic interference**. We understand a word to have a certain meaning but the other person has a different meaning. Body language and gestures mean different things to different people. This includes confusion of abbreviated organizational jargon and pronunciation. Universal meanings (semantic understanding) are rare.

- **Syntactic interference**. Words are placed in certain order to give our language meaning. If the words are out of order, the meaning may be changed (this includes grammar).

- ■ **Organizational interference.** Ideas being discussed lack sequence and can't be followed.

- ■ **Psychological interference.** Words that incite emotion are used. In any emotional state (positive or negative) emotions need to be diffused in order to communicate effectively.

- ■ **Social interference.** This includes cultural manners that are inappropriate for the country such as accepted codes for dress, business etiquette, communication rules, social activity.

Always become well informed about the customs and culture and get information before you try and do business in another country. Review this book and decide which areas of communication you and your colleagues will have difficulty with in China. Anticipate and plan accordingly.

As the visitor to another country, you need to move out of your "comfort zone." Make the people from another country feel comfortable doing business with you.

No one country has a lock on world markets. Fundamental changes have occurred in the world economy in the last decade. New technologies, and low labor costs often give nations that once were not major players an advantage. This results in increased competition. Yet international business is vital to any country's prosperity.

Business is conducted by people and the future of any country in a global economy will lie with people who can effectively think and act across ethnic, cultural and language barriers. We need to understand that the differences between nations and cultures is profound. The European-based culture of the United States has very different values and behaviors than other cultures in the world. If you cannot accept and adapt to these differences, you will not succeed.

Companies striving to market their business overseas can become truly successful only when they recognize that the key is operating with sensitivity toward the culture and communication of the other country. Communication cannot be separated from culture and this is true when doing business in other countries.

No flourishing company would present themselves to another company in their own country without researching that company's business culture and then adapting their image to meet the customer's comfort level. It's the same when doing business in another country. You must adapt your image by using your knowledge of effective cultural communication to present a positive public image to the other country.

The first thing is to identify your target audience: clients, customers, suppliers, financial people, government employees and so on. Then you must learn how to effectively communication with them and this means learning the culture.

Business failure internationally rarely results from technical or professional incompetence. It is often due to a lack of understanding of what people from other countries want, how they work and so on. This lack of understanding can put a company at a tremendous disadvantage.

Learning the business protocol and practices of the country where you want to do business can give you great leverage. The more you know about the people you do business with, the more successful you can be. Businesspeople must make every contact they have with a foreign customer or business partner a positive one. Business leaders and managers must rethink the way they do business in the new global marketplace.

To succeed in the global market, you must:

- **Be flexible.** Cultural adaptations are necessary for both countries to get along and do business. Resisting the local culture will only lead to distrust.

- **Be patient.** Adjust your planning. Initiating business in many countries takes a long-range approach and may require two or three years. Anticipate problems and develop alternative strategies.

- **Prepare thoroughly.** Research the country, the organization, the culture and beliefs of the people you will be dealing with.

- **Know your bottom line.** Know exactly what you want from a deal and at what point an agreement is not in your best interest. Know when to walk away.

- **Keep your cool.** Pay attention to the wide range of national, cultural, religious and social differences you encounter.

- **Form relationships.** Encourage getting involved with the new community if your a going to be in the country for a long period.

- **Show respect.** Search for the other side's needs and interests. Accentuate the positive. Don't preach your own beliefs, and respect their beliefs..

When you are using this booklet, review your own beliefs and values about correct business protocol and ethics. Then match these ideas with the business practices and protocol in China.

You can contribute to your own success by recognizing that you will have to move out of your own "comfort zone" of doing business into the cultural business zone of China in order to develop the rapport necessary to meet the needs of your client or partner. This does not mean you compromise your company's image or product but that you do business following China's protocol while there. It's only for a short time that you may be following their rules and the payoff can be one in which concepts can be sold while still maintaining a consistent image and approach that is culturally appropriate.

Quick Tips: China

- Be patient and persistent. Things take a lot longer than in the U.S. Observe rather than talk.. Be friendly and sincere.

- Don't say anything in English you don't want heard. Many Chinese can write and understand English.

- Translate as much of your written material as possible ahead of time; if you let the Chinese do it, you lose control and time.

- Being successful in China has little to do with the merit of your product; the important thing is the relationships established. Send the same person each time.

- If you run afoul of the authorities, remember that logic doesn't work. Apologize.

- Use your own interpreters so that you are sure that you understand all agreements.

- The Chinese love to come to America. Give yourself the home court advantage if possible and invite them to come to the U.S.

- Focus on how you can help China modernize. Play down any benefits to your firm. Also it helps to convey the impression you are anxious to help China progress technologically.

- A major objective of the Chinese is obtaining Western technology but they do not want to spend their limited hard currency buying Western goods. They want to learn how to manufacture high tech goods themselves. They often buy Western goods in order to learn the technology. They also want Western sales presentations to contain as much technical information as they can get. Know how much technology you are willing to give.

- The Chinese do not have the same attitude toward intellectual property rights that exist in Western countries. Therefore, they do not protect these rights. Always remember this before deciding what information to give.

- Chinese workers must be taught exactly what to look for. They must be taught how to use and service equipment and this training must be ongoing.

- To establish a business in China you must do it on their terms. This means finding skilled business and professional people, training them to your specifications, and then letting the Chinese build and run the operation with your role being one of supervision.

The respelling of Mandarin is done for ease of pronunciation for English speakers. Chinese is a tonal language which means there are four basic tones in pronunciation. The change in pitch is on the vowel, and by changing the pitch on many words, the meaning is changed.

The pitches are: 1. a high flat pitch (‒), 2. rises from mid to high pitch (∕), 3. drops from mid-low to low pitch and then rises to mid-high pitch (∨), 4. falls from high to low pitch (∖).

The *Ts* is pronouned like the ts in "its."

Good morning	Tsou-en
Good afternoon	Woo-en
Good evening	Wahn-en
Goodbye	Tsi jen
My name is...	Waw duh ming Zshur
What's your name?	Nee duh ming Zshur
How are you?	Nee How Maw
Fine (good)	How
Thank you	Shee-eh, shee-eh
You are welcome	Boo-kuh-chee

Excuse me	Dway-boo-chee
Please	Ching
Yes	Tshua-j shoo
No	Boo
Mr.	Shen shun
Mrs.	Tai Tai
Miss	Shou jeh

Available in this series:

Business China

Business France

Business Germany

Business Japan

Business Mexico

Business Taiwan

For more information, please contact:

Sales and Marketing Department
NTC Publishing Group
4255 West Touhy Avenue
Lincolnwood, IL 60646
708-679-5500